The Easter Story Hidden Pictures
Activity Book

Story based on the four Gospels: Matthew, Mark, Luke, and John

Written by: **Robin Loisch**

Illustrated by: **Chad Thompson**

Scripture quotation taken from The Holy Bible, New International Version® NIV® Copyright © 1973, 1978, 1984, 2011 by Biblica, Inc. Used with permission. All rights reserved worldwide.

The purchase of this coloring book grants you the rights to photocopy the contents for classroom use. Notice: It is unlawful to copy these pages for resale purposes. Copy permission is for private use only.

Copyright © 2025 Warner Press, Inc. All rights reserved. Made in USA

Jesus went to Jerusalem for the Passover celebration.
The people were so happy to see Him.
They waved palm branches and shouted, "Hosanna!"

Find the hidden pictures: gift, doughnut, heart, drink cup, worm, piece of cake, crescent moon, bandage, fish, and flag.

The chief priests were very angry when they saw
how the people loved Jesus.
They began to plan a way to kill Him.

Find the hidden pictures: check mark, football, rainbow, volleyball, chameleon, ice cream cone, mug, spaceship, Christmas tree, and pencil.

Judas, one of Jesus' disciples, asked the chief priests, "What will you give me if I help you catch Jesus?" The men gave Judas 30 silver coins.

Find the hidden pictures: slice of pizza, paintbrush, puzzle piece, banana, popsicle, orange slice, rainbow, camera, paper boat, and heart.

Jesus and His disciples ate a special
Passover meal together.

Find the hidden pictures: whale, balloon, cat, birdhouse, bone, bowl, carrot, feather, crab, and mountains.

Jesus told the disciples many things.
Then He shared the bread and wine with them.
"Whenever you eat the bread and drink the wine, remember Me," Jesus said.

Find the hidden pictures: kite, heart, diamond, watermelon slice, lightning bolt, book, envelope, pencil, tooth, and doughnut.

At the Mount of Olives, Jesus told His disciples they would soon leave Him. "I will not leave You!" Peter said. "Before the rooster crows twice, you will disown Me three times," Jesus replied.

Find the hidden pictures: wine glass, fish, mushroom, rocket, paintbrush, heart, clock, strawberry, arrow, balloon, and banana.

Jesus went to the garden of Gethsemane to pray.
Then Judas came, bringing men with swords and clubs to capture Him.

Find the hidden pictures: cat, heart, strawberry, candle, tulip, mushroom, lightbulb, umbrella, ruler, and diamond.

Jesus was taken to Pilate to be judged.
Pilate knew Jesus had done nothing wrong.
"What should I do with Jesus?" he asked. "CRUCIFY HIM!" the people shouted.

Find the hidden pictures: envelope, sun, moon, bananas, turtle, paintbrush, crown, sock, slice of pizza, candy, and frying pan.

Soldiers took Jesus away. They dressed Him in a purple robe
like a king, made fun of Him, and hit Him.
Then they made a crown of thorns and pushed it down on His head.

**Find the hidden pictures: bandage, birdhouse, mug, banana, rainbow,
paintbrush, thermometer, heart, bone, and puzzle piece.**

They made Jesus carry a heavy wooden cross to Golgotha, which means "the place of the skull." They nailed Him to the cross and put it between the crosses of two thieves.

Find the hidden pictures: candle, doughnut, whale, lightbulb, carrot, heart, box, moon, bandaid, and envelope.

The sky grew dark. Jesus cried out in a loud voice and died. At that moment the temple curtain was torn in two, and the earth shook. A Roman centurion said, "Surely He was the Son of God!"

Find the hidden pictures: book, kite, pencil, ruler, French fries, diamond, check mark, mug, ghost, and crab.

Joseph of Arimathea took Jesus' body,
wrapped it in clean cloth, and laid it in his own new tomb.
Then he rolled a big stone in front of the door and left.

Find the hidden pictures: cat, piece of cake, drink cup, teapot, fish, lady bug, umbrella, ice cream cone, hamburger, and worm.

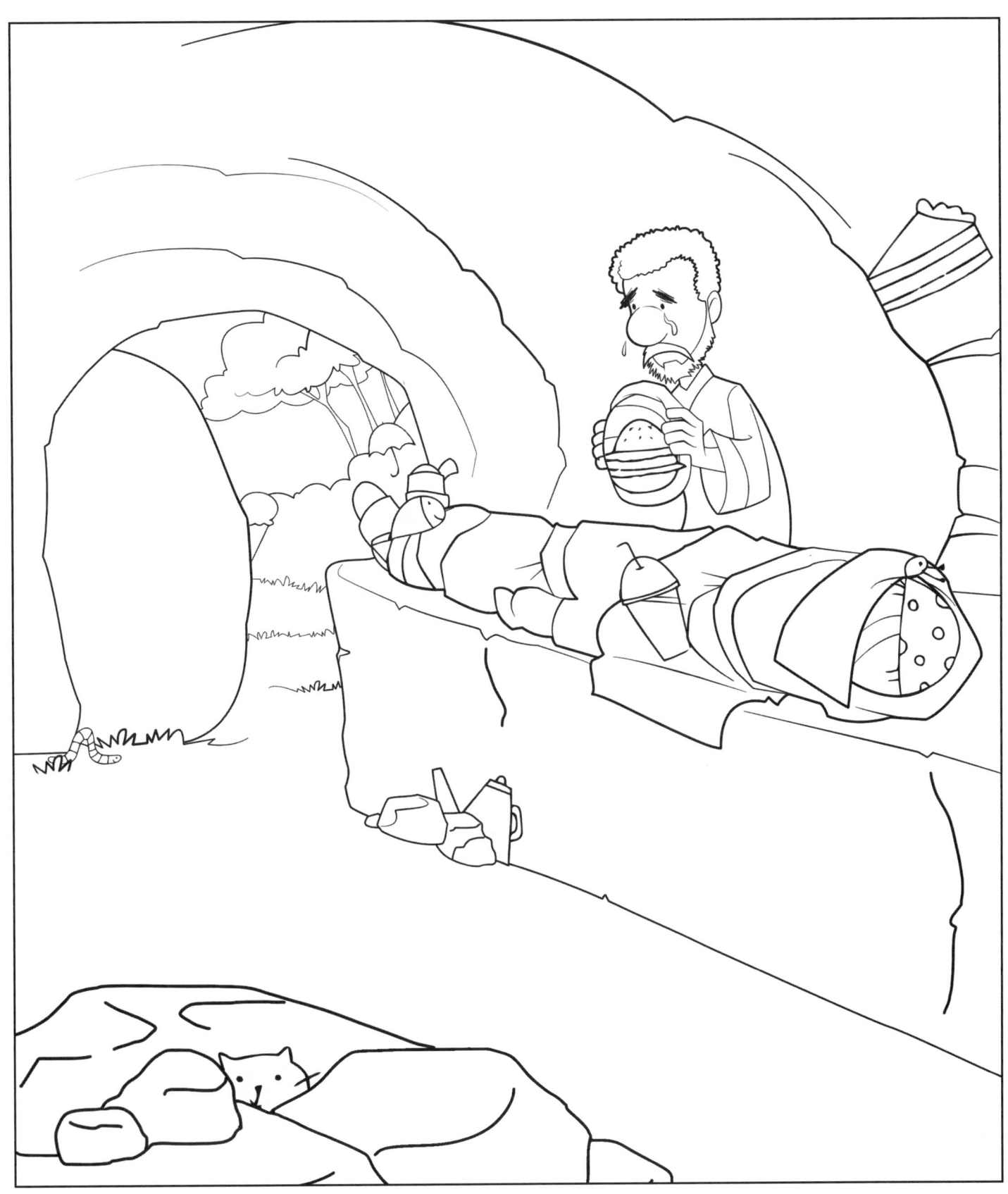

Pilate sent guards to watch the tomb. Three days later, the guards felt a terrible earthquake and saw an angel roll away the stone and sit on it. They were so scared they fainted!

Find the hidden pictures: feather, tulip, check mark, basketball, carrot, envelope, slice of pizza, paper airplane, umbrella, and a smiley flower.

Two of Jesus' friends came to the tomb. The stone was rolled away! The angel said, "Jesus has risen!" Then the women ran to tell the disciples.

Find the hidden pictures: slice of pizza, lightning bolt, ghost, mountains, bananas, mug, check mark, paper boat, paintbrush, and cup.

Later, Jesus met with His disciples and showed them the nail scars in His hands and feet. Then He went up to heaven. The disciples told everyone, "Jesus is alive!"

Find the hidden pictures: paintbrush, spaceship, rainbow, banana, lightning bolt, leaf, flag, heart, popsicle, and paper boat.

He has risen, just as he said.
MATTHEW 28:6 (NIV)